A Leisure Journal

- DIARY • POEMS
- PAINTINGS

Activities to inspire you

Poems by Linda Wilton
Illustrations by Myrtle Paterson

A Leisure Journal

Copyright © Linda Wilton and Myrtle Paterson 2012
The rights of Linda Wilton to be identified as the author
and Myrtle Paterson as illustrator of this work
have been asserted by them in accordance with the
Copyright, Designs and Patents Act 1988.

ISBN: 978-1-907636-48-6

All rights reserved. No part of this publication may be
reproduced or transmitted in any form or by any means,
electronic or mechanical, including photocopying, recording,
or any information storage and retrieval system without
permission in writing from the author.

Published by Verité CM Ltd
for Linda Wilton and Myrtle Paterson

British Library Cataloguing Data
A catalogue record of this book is available from
The British Library

Typesetting and production management by
Verité CM Ltd, Worthing, West Sussex UK
+44 (0) 1903 241975
Printed in The Czech Republic

Introduction

We have all heard it said that "All work and no play makes Jack a dull boy". With hundreds of possible leisure activities and hobbies, life need never be dull.

This journal will help you keep track of those special leisure dates, anniversaries, and memorable occasions that are all too soon forgotten.

Hopefully, amongst the varied activities, you will see something new you would like to try. Everyone has talent of some sort, but not all are in a position, either financially or geographically, to nurture or develop it, but we can all 'have a go' at something.

This book of appropriate and thoughtful poems, composed by Linda Wilton, and beautifully illustrated by her sister, Myrtle Paterson, will, I am sure, inspire you to 'have a go' at something new and find unexpected pleasure and fulfilment. Maybe it will leave a special event you wish to record and look back on.

Biography

Myrtle and Linda are sisters who grew up in Worthing. With both parents and grandparents in the horticultural industry, it is not surprising that they both inherited a love of all things natural, and over the years they nurtured a passion for wild life.

With art and music of various forms being enjoyed within the family, these talents developed in different directions in the two daughters.

Myrtle took up floristry and painting, exhibiting and selling at various venues. She is an active member of Watford and Bushey Art Society, and has been a winner of The Roy Chaffin Challenge Trophy. She has also been a finalist several times in the 'Paint a Wildlife Subject' (PAWS) competitions.

Biography

Linda's talents lie within music and poetry. Her poems have been published in various anthologies produced by 'Poetry Now'. She has also written for the West Sussex Gazette and Corfe Valley News, finding her greatest inspiration in beautiful areas of landscape.

She was nominated a Distinguished Member of the International Society of Poets in 1988.

Having combined their gifts to produce previous books 'On Watford's Wild Side' and later 'Enchanting Brownsea' for the John Lewis Partnership, they have now concentrated their thoughts on leisure activities and have designed this journal around poems and paintings, to enable the reader to keep a record of especially happy events.

Leisure Topics

JANUARY	Doing puzzles	10
	Fun in the snow	12
	Friendship	14
FEBRUARY	Story telling	24
	Making music	26
	Knitting and Sewing	28
MARCH	Painting	38
	Keeping pets	40
	Gardening	42
APRIL	Bird-watching	52
	Jogging	54
	Kite-flying and wind sports	56
MAY	Fishing	66
	Dog walking	68
	Ball games	70
JUNE	Golfing	80
	Photography	82
	Taking aim	84

Leisure Topics

JULY	Picnicking	94
	Water sports	96
	Barbecuing	98
AUGUST	Building sandcastles	108
	Hill walking	110
	Lazing	112
SEPTEMBER	Reflecting	122
	Fun on wheels	124
	Preserving	126
OCTOBER	Taking tea	136
	Watching TV	138
	Model making	140
NOVEMBER	Reading	150
	Singing	152
	Busking	154
DECEMBER	Star gazing	164
	Going to the pantomime	166
	Christmas	168

A Leisure Journal

Winter Walk

When we have left the cosy hearth
To take a walk through woodland path,
And all wrapped up against the chill
We seek the trees that skirt the hill.

We find amidst the shelter there
A time to walk without a care.
To ponder on the whispering wind,
As noises from the town are dimmed.

To watch the branches shake and sway,
Their dormant buds await the day
When stirrings in the trunk below
Alert them once again to grow.

The catkins mimmick lambs' tails soft
With pollen shaken, borne aloft
By winds that make the branches sway.
Oh, what a lovely winter's day!

The moss, new-sprung of verdant green
That camouflages all that's seen
From trunk to twig to cast its cloak,
Transforming rubbish dropped by folk.

And ivy clambers, twists and twirls
As skyward up the tree it curls.
The cuckoo-pint, now inches tall,
Pierces the leaves of last year's fall.

So many lovely things are here.
Who says the winter can't bring cheer?
As through the woods our path we trace
And revel in its stark embrace.

January

January

Puzzling

I wonder why, when winding down,
And sitting in my dressing gown,
Before I toddle off to bed
I like to tax my little head.

Whatever puzzles in the day
Have inconveniently come my way.
I like to solve another sort
Of brain teasers – my mental sport.

It might be word search, crosswords too,
Or simple tasks of 'How to do'.
Then jigsaws try my patience more,
Or scrabbling for the highest score.
(And what's that piece still on the floor?)

My I.Q. never has been great.
And sudoku – it's just too late
For mathematic skills to tease
My little brain cells – simpler please!

Perhaps leave two across undone,
Its clue a quite ambiguous pun.
As slumber overtakes my eyes
I've missed the deadline for a prize!

January

The missing letters of the alphabet spell the name of which T.V. programme?

Make each box and each column contain six different shapes

Each box and each row must contain the numbers 1 to 9

Answers to puzzles: Beginortshu: Neighbours Dorrsowes: Crossword Buerbdckin: Rubikcube Asundieng: Mindgames Gaphyltin: Plaything

11

A Leisure Journal

The Snow

When fierce and freezing blows the wind
And huddled figures brave the blast.
Eager to welcome heavier skies
That herald snow to fall at last.

Then all seems peaceful, muffled, quiet,
As white and soft the snowflakes fall.
And children squeal with cold delight
Whilst scooping snowballs from the wall.

I watch the lone bird seek for crumbs,
Its tiny footprints traced in snow.
And my dog rolls in ecstasy,
He's longing for a walk to go.

Up to the hills where drifts have formed
And sculptured ledges make us climb.
Where unexpected depths appear
Beneath our weight at melting time.

The anxious drive on icy roads
Can overshadow our delight
At wondering at this pure white form
Which thrills the sense of sound and sight.

January

Friendship

My mate called round the other day
With grapes and lucozade.
He'd heard I was in bed with flu
And rushed to give me aid.

Recovery seemed oh! so long,
His phone calls kept me sane.
His kindness gladly I'll repay
If ever he's in pain.

Our tastes are very much the same
That's why we get along.
He's got the guts to tell me if
I'm doing something wrong.

If ever I am lonely
Or I'm near depression's brink,
I know he'll gladly join me
For a chat over a drink.

We'll wander to the Rose and Crown,
And there, over a beer
He'll put things in perspective, so
Dispelling all my fear.

We're mates you see, and friends like that
Are worth much more than gold.
So all life's ups and downs we'll share
Until we both grow old.

January

A Leisure Journal

1st January

2nd January

3rd January

4th January

5th January

6th January

7th January

8th January

9th January

10th January

11th January

12th January

13th January

14th January

A Leisure Journal

15th January

16th January

17th January

18th January

19th January

20th January

21st January

January

22nd January

23rd January

24th January

25th January

26th January

27th January

28th January

A Leisure Journal

29th January

30th January

31st January

Notes

January

Notes

February Fog

Soft, damp, absorbing cloak,
Muffling sounds and sight,
Fog-drops form and poise on twigs,
Quiet as the night.

Hillside kine sound eerie,
Lost to view but near,
Beyond the new horizons,
Teasing eye and ear.

Everything distorted
In the damp white mist.
Intermittent blindness lurks
At each bend and twist.

With creeping silent stealth you fill the hollows.
A stubborn and impenetrable blanket,
Until the sun and wind contrive together
To sear and blow the fog away – Nun danket!

February

February

A Leisure Journal

Story Time

Daddy, please tell me a story.
I've been waiting ever so long.
You said you would come after bath-time.
But that was at seven, so what's wrong?

I know that you like to watch telly
While Mummy and I splash about.
But I'm dried, and waiting in bed now,
And I've got my favourite book out.

I've stories of fairies and dragons,
And creatures that fill me with fright.
But when your arm's wrapped all around me
I know everything is alright.

So Daddy, please read me my story,
And when all my prayers are said
I promise I'll be very quiet,
And stay all tucked up in my bed.

February

Music

The melody has stopped me in my tracks
And moved me so to silence my routine.
Halted, I thus felt the sound rush through me
And strange emotions stirred where none had been.

A double-bass now quivered through my spine.
Ethereal choirs – which made the tears to flow.
So physically mastered by the sound
And spiritually touched, I now let go…

Into the unseen world of symphony
Created by the mastery of man,
To seek those feelings buried in the depths,
With wave on wave of sound, had been the plan.

Never discordant trash could seek me thus,
My ear rebels against the jangling din.
But this, perfection of musician's art
To me, with senses heightened, entered in.

Thank God for beauty that has such power,
Through man's harmonious skills of voice and string,
To stop, transfix and transform every part
Into a nobler being, or better thing.

February

Knit-Nattering

Nan's fingers are deft.
She's the only one left
With time to knit-natter most days.
There are scarves, blankets, ties,
And warm wraps for cold thighs.
With what patience and calm she displays.

Now Grandpa is crafty
And just for a laugh, he
Knocked up a doll's house of wood,
With matchsticks and gum
That would dry in the sun.
For a plaything, 'twas misunderstood.

Unlike dear Nan's patterns
Which outlive the fashions
Of each family member alike.
Grandpa's doll's house was fragile.
Us kids were too agile.
It collapsed with the very first strike!

February

A Leisure Journal

1st February

2nd February

3rd February

4th February

5th February

6th February

7th February

February

8th February

9th February

10th February

11th February

12th February

13th February

14th February

A Leisure Journal

15th February

16th February

17th February

18th February

19th February

20th February

21st February

February

22nd February

23rd February

24th February

25th February

26th February

27th February

28th February

A Leisure Journal

29th February

Notes

February

Notes

Uncertain Spring

"Dare I come out?" I hear the snowdrop say.
"With death I seem to dice
  To push up through the ice.
  Dare I come out?"

"Dare I come out?" I hear the primrose say.
"Those eager hands will want to pick.
  To see the sun I must be quick.
  Dare I come out?"

"Dare I come out?" I hear the bluebell say.
"Too soon I shall be trampled underfoot,
  No care is taken where the boot is put.
  Dare I come out?"

"Let's chance it" I hear a thoughtful whisper from the buds.
"We should encourage humans to show willing
  From dreary winter into action springing.
  Yes, let's come out!"

March

Big-head or What!

Give me a brush and can of paint.
Give me a box of tiles.
A book of wallpaper to choose
From differing kinds of styles.
If it's a thorough job you want,
Or if it's just a lick
Of paint required, my work you'll find
Is really rather slick.
I also like to paint with oils
The subjects in my mind.
Expressing on a canvas small,
Art of a different kind.
My home is testimony to
My artistic incline.
Whatever walls need sprucing up,
You'll see my talent shine!

March

The Home-comings

He sought Puss in the garden shed,
In hall and lounge and under bed.
Well, lonely cat could not be found
Despite Bill searching all around.
He checked 'neath cars in roadway wide,
There pussy sometimes liked to hide.
But, listening to Bill's frantic call
The cat hid 'neath the neighbour's wall.
Fed up with being left alone,
Puss went and found another home.

A fussy independent 'mog',
Puss wasn't faithful, like a dog.
Companionship was what he chose,
Yet loneliness made him morose.
He'd love a cuddle on Bill's lap,
And in his garden take a nap.
But since Bill's been away for days,
Now on the neighbour's lawn he'll laze.

He'll stretch his claws and yawn and roll.
See what's put in his special bowl.
He's learnt to climb the window sill
And find a bed if he feels ill.
Bill's neighbour finds the cat a joy.
A special furry, silver boy.
She's glad to fuss him every day,
Not JUST when Bill's on holiday.

March

The Joys of Gardening

Digging weeds.
Aching back.
Humping soil.
Clearing track.
Pruning bushes.
Killing slugs.
Spreading muck.
Filling trugs.
Twisting wires.
Trimming edges.
Planting borders.
Clipping hedges.
Sweeping leaves.
Sweat and toil.
Cuts and bruises.
Stony soil.
Killing blight.
Pretty sight.
Now sit back – admire the view.
Joys of gardening coming true.

March

A Leisure Journal

1st March

2nd March

3rd March

4th March

5th March

6th March

7th March

March

8th March

9th March

10th March

11th March

12th March

13th March

14th March

A Leisure Journal

15th March

16th March

17th March

18th March

19th March

20th March

21st March

March

22nd March

23rd March

24th March

25th March

26th March

27th March

28th March

A Leisure Journal

29th March

30th March

31st March

Notes

March

Notes

Just Before Seven

Expressing in words, an impossible task –
This scene of Heaven,
Just before seven,
As in fading sunlight the landscape is basked.

Such artistic displays make me wonder with awe
How colours are made
During twilight and shade.
To heighten our sense is what beauty is for.

The bright golden disc is descending the sky,
Transforming the blues
To unparalleled hues,
Which night's spreading mantle will fade by and by.

Would that some of our partings could leave such a mark.
Glorious farewells,
Leaving their spells
On the void and the silence that falls after dark.

Bright orange and violet, with streaks of blood red.
Clouds in a cacoon
Of pink and maroon.
The sun's parting gift as it pops off to bed.

So cherish each sunset, until the bright hour
When, turning in space
We come face to face
With the dawning of light and its strengthening power.

April

Watching the Bird House

The thrushes told the starlings
That somewhere in a tree
They'd seen a little bird-house
Where they could live for free.
The starlings found the residence
Hanging on a hook.
The surroundings were so pretty that
They thought they'd take a look.
The entrance hole was tiny and
They couldn't squeeze inside.
Oh dear! A disadvantage when
You quickly want to hide.
A pretty little tawny owl
Flew round to view it next,
But he couldn't get his head inside
So hooted "Well I'm vexed".
Next came a jay, all pink and blue.
"No, no", she squawked, "This just won't do".
A lesser-spotted woodpecker
Then flew around to call.
But when he tried to look inside
He didn't fit at all.
A blue-tit was the last to see
The little bird-house in the tree.
She needed somewhere safe to lay
Her eggs which might come any day.
She found the little house a treat.
Her blue-tit heart fair skipped a beat.
The house was sheltered from the cold.
The FOR SALE sign was changed to SOLD.
I've seen this saga played each Spring.
What pleasure watching birds can bring.

April

Jogging

I'm leaving the road where the park gates once stood.
Seems an awful long way over hills to the wood.
Won't stop at the cafe, a magnet for me
Can't wait to pop in on my way back for tea.

I'm over the top where the view broadens out.
There are usually several dog-walkers about
Where a short path traverses the one that I've climbed.
To rest is the one thing that I have in mind!

A quick jog round woods that seem airless and cold,
To visit here after dark, 'ghostly' I'm told.
But soon I'm descending in more ways than one
As the path has got muddy to add to my fun.

So, 'plastered' and aching I puff and I pant,
Though my special jog outfit is really quite scant.
Crossing cornfields and ditches, along a tight lane.
I skirt round a golf course to woodland again.

'Tis only the sight of the cafe in view
Keeps me going with thoughts of its welcoming brew!
I'm tired and I'm aching – hurrah for my tea.
But to jog is one pleasure in life that is FREE.

April

The Squall

Have you encountered springtime squalls
When, stripped and whipped the blossom falls
Confetti-like upon the lawn,
And pine-cones from their branches torn
Come clattering down to bounce around
The soft pine needles on the ground?

All efforts by the birds are vain.
They try to soar, yet held by chains
Their wings beat madly 'gainst the gale,
But prisoner-like, their efforts fail.
Like paper darts and kites on strings
The terns swoop down with swept-back wings.

Despite the wind and choppy waves
Wind-surfers purposefully brave
The current on a rising tide
And revel in a bumpy ride.
A firm grip's needed for the kite.
A gust can whisk it out of sight.

The yachts are struggling in the gale,
With clapping, flapping, tearing sail
They keel and bounce, a dangerous ride
As occupants hang overside.
A lonely water-skier, tense
Bounces back home if he has sense.

With dust and sand and leaves whipped up,
Grit fills the sandwiches and cup.
Meanwhile the children on the beach
Squeal as they jump out of waves' reach.
Picnics are quickly packed away.
There'll always be another day.

April

A Leisure Journal

1st April

2nd April

3rd April

4th April

5th April

6th April

7th April

April

8th April

9th April

10th April

11th April

12th April

13th April

14th April

A Leisure Journal

15th April

16th April

17th April

18th April

19th April

20th April

21st April

April

22nd April

23rd April

24th April

25th April

26th April

27th April

28th April

A Leisure Journal

29th April

30th April

Notes

April

Notes

The Maytime Suit

The buds have burst their final coats,
And chestnut gowns adorn the green
With spikes of flower – their lavish blooms,
Such beauty here in Maytime seen.
The bluebells dense, in soft blue dress
Ring out "It's Spring" upon the breeze.
With subtle scent they fill the air.
Their message carries through the trees.

Intense and lush are Spring's new robes,
Mantles not made by human hand.
Intrinsic blossoms need no thread,
Just warmth and showers to nourish land,
So that creation starts again.
From bud to flower, and flower to fruit,
And fruit to seed… to rest till May,
Waiting to don a new Spring suit.

May

May

The Lone Fisherman

I've been out here since half-past nine,
Eager to try my rod and line.
So far I've caught three lovely bass,
Four mackerel and one smallish wrasse.

Whilst fishing boats go speeding by,
Accompanied by seagulls' cry.
They dive and soar around each boat
Returning from depths more remote...

I'm happy in my own small way
To fish in a relaxing way.
I like to lose myself in thought,
Not get obsessed with what I've caught.

My mind has set the world aright.
To sit and fish is sheer delight,
And watch the busy world float by,
Or contemplate the changing sky.

Out here upon the jetty small
I feel the currents ebb and thrall,
And hope my tasty bit of bait
Will finalise the fish's fate!

I heard it told the other day
A lovely mermaid passed this way
With golden hair and silver scales.
That sure excited all the males!

But that was many moons ago,
When sandbanks altered tidal flow.
And yet, just then, far out to sea
A graceful arm was beckoning me!!!

Oh dear – I've been here far too long.
The sun upon my head is strong.
I'll leave my mermaid to the sea
And head back home to sanity.

May

Awakening

Fresh, newly sprung the virgin green,
Black branches still show through
The woodland trees. Whilst on the ground
Thick carpets of rich blue.

Cow parsley spatters every hedge.
Anemones still linger
With up-turned heads towards the sun,
The Spring's early harbinger.

The primrose spills upon the bank
Its simple yellow flowers.
And nestling near the blackthorn's root
The little violet cowers.

So unforgettable this sight
As wakening woods rejoice.
And birds encapsulate it all
With their exultant voice.

I sit and ponder Spring's return,
How silent is its working.
But my dog's only interest is
What 'neath each bush is lurking!

May

Ball Games

Think of a world without a ball,
Doesn't seem quite right at all.
Whether pitch or court or green,
Many different balls are seen.

Kicked up skywards 'twixt two poles.
Being clubbed down earthy holes.

Weighted ones to hit a Jack,
Bowled in hopes they'll not curve back.

"Come on mate, that's just not cricket."
"Only aiming for your wicket!"

Clonked with mallets through the hoops.
Forwards, sideways, round the loops.

Kicked and punched and knocked around.
Rolling miles along the ground.

To and fro across a net.
Shouts of, "Love, game, deuce or set".

I'd not like to be a ball,
Often thumped against a wall.
Who I'd hit, or how I'm caught.
Talk about a life that's fraught.
Never knowing where I'd fall.
I'm so glad I'm not a ball!

May

A Leisure Journal

1st May

2nd May

3rd May

4th May

5th May

6th May

7th May

May

8th May

9th May

10th May

11th May

12th May

13th May

14th May

A Leisure Journal

15th May

16th May

17th May

18th May

19th May

20th May

21st May

May

22nd May

23rd May

24th May

25th May

26th May

27th May

28th May

A Leisure Journal

29th May

30th May

31st May

Notes

May

Notes

Afloat

The cruisers cut through floating weed,
Their engines purr along the creek.
A paradise afloat they seek,
Some lazing, some preferring speed.

Each quacking group, a picture pose
Of ducks, perturbed by wayward oar,
But moorhens stay on weedy tor,
No fear to show as we glide close.

The minute baby ducks can move
So fast to stay by mother's side
Whilst they're endeavouring to hide.
Such trust their fluffy forms can prove.

And all around the air so clear.
The wispy willow's watery bower
Provides the shelter in the shower.
And peace is broken by the weir.

No traffic fumes or clangour fill
Our new-discovered shady banks.
On lonely seat we whisper thanks
Where darting kingfisher can thrill.

We look around at wrinkled bark
And dipping fronds. The cone-filled arm
Rests on the green, – I feel no harm
Could even reach me after dark.

June

June

Hole in One

Driven by the desire to win
The golfer's aim – to hit the pin.
The course begins on velvet tees,
Secure, we drive, with stylish ease.
But confidence is soon cut short,
And this is where we enter 'sport'.

To stay on 'fairway', smooth and green,
When the odd dog-leg can be seen,
Or steer through bunkers, left and right.
Their steep sides an unwelcome sight.
And keeping off the rough terrain.
This concentration is a strain.

But here we are, come rain or shine,
To start our game at half-past nine.
Precision and patience rule our sport,
To drive and putt as we've been taught.
What started out as earnest fun
Has now produced a 'hole in one!'

So, drinks all round, at end of play.
For us a memorable day.

June

Focusing

The smallest object, far away
I see with ease upon a day
When focusing with steady hand,
I aim to scour the sea and land.

I spot such rare and lovely things;
A migrant bird, preening its wings,
A far off gypsy caravan,
Or moors and hills untouched by man.

I'd like to make a calendar
To send to friends both near and far.
Lighting and composition make
The very best shots I can take.

Each picture taken through the lens
Of landscapes, objects or my friends.
A memory fine for days to come,
To ponder with a scrap-book chum.

June

Every Day's a Bonus

As dawn creeps o'er the window sill
I ponder on life's meaning still.
Is it a chance to right some wrong,
Or in adversity, be strong?
A chance to practice, train and learn,
A moment of respect to earn?
To shoot a goal, to have an aim,
To conquer fear, discover fame?
So many chances each day brings
To let your hidden dreams take wings.
Have I the time to understand
If life was 'accident' or 'planned'?
We think, we pray, sometimes beguile,
And offer friendship with a smile.
Each one of us can play our part
To warm this poor world's coldest heart.

June

A Leisure Journal

1st June

2nd June

3rd June

4th June

5th June

6th June

7th June

June

8th June

9th June

10th June

11th June

12th June

13th June

14th June

A Leisure Journal

15th June

16th June

17th June

18th June

19th June

20th June

21st June

June

22nd June

23rd June

24th June

25th June

26th June

27th June

28th June

A Leisure Journal

29th June

30th June

Notes

June

Notes

Summer Heat

Frail is the summer flower
That blossoms and withers in the hedge,
Its petals scorched by mid-day sun
Once drenched by morning dew,
Its nectar, life-blood to the bee.

High-noon, and dust obliterates the verges.
Unable to discard their fur or feathers
Creatures pant as they seek shade,
Lying motionless, apart from flicking
Away the nuisance flies.

Man plods on in the heat,
Sweat discolouring the rim of his hat
And running down his brow.
Each task takes twice as long,
Each step takes twice the effort.

Just as the summer flower
He flourishes, withers and dies…
His life-blood spent
And his skin cracked and decayed.
Stifled, he is gone.

July

July

93

The Picnic

With a wasp on the jam tart, a fly in our tea.
Oh! the joys of a picnic for my family and me.

But nothing could spoil our repast in the sun.
And finding a spot had been ever such fun.

We'd scrambled through sand-dunes, and hiked over stiles.
We'd followed the sea-shore considerable miles

Until, where the view had been one of the best
We spread out our picnic and stopped for a rest.

There were strawberries and cheesecake, ham rolls and fresh scones.
With nibbles and crisps and some lovely ripe 'toms'.

Oh! what a spread, what a treat for the eye.
So with tummies now full we lay under the sky.

The hamper is empty, the packets likewise.
Amazing how eating outdoors satisfies!

July

Respect

Water, rolling, splashing, swelling,
Source of power and yet in-dwelling.
Changing shore-lines, flooding plains.
Thankfully men thought of drains.

Dams still harness water's power.
Some mills past their finest hour.
Man's recreation features more
In what he uses water for.

There's boating, fishing, swimming too,
A luxury bathroom (and a loo!).
New railways being driven by steam.
Materialisation of old dreams.

Diviner's art – water, you speak
To landscapes that are void and bleak.
And say in rhythms, quenching thirst,
"Respect me, for God made me first."

So as you watch the sea close by,
Reflecting all that's in the sky,
Remember, when you sit and muse,
Just how much water we all use.

July

The Barbecue

Come on, let's have a barbecue
The village dads all said.
Our Reg can make the burgers,
And I'll provide the bread.

I've several bags of charcoal
All stored up in my shed.
There should be quite enough to see
That everyone is fed.

The mums can make some salads
And all kinds of fancy sweets.
I'm sure the grans and grandads
Can rustle up some treats.

We'll light up fairly early
So the coals get hot and red.
We want it to be over 'fore
The kiddies go to bed.

We'll put the word out quickly,
Before the sun is set.
The weather forecast's looking good –
Not likely to be wet.

July

A Leisure Journal

1st July

2nd July

3rd July

4th July

5th July

6th July

7th July

July

8th July

9th July

10th July

11th July

12th July

13th July

14th July

A Leisure Journal

15th July

16th July

17th July

18th July

19th July

20th July

21st July

July

22nd July

23rd July

24th July

25th July

26th July

27th July

28th July

A Leisure Journal

29th July

30th July

31st July

Notes

July

Notes

Harvest Festival

Combines clatter through the ripened corn.
Reapers busy since the light of dawn.
Husky dust fills the August air.
Animals flee, to hide elsewhere.

The hedgerows fill with the harmless mice,
Escaping the strokes of the combine vice.
Leaving stubble to be ploughed back in.
Thank God for the end result – bread for my bin!

The children ring the steeple bells
That welcome all to gather in
And praise the One Creator God
With voices raised in much-loved hymns.

With harvest vegetables piled up high
Across the choir stalls. Now the sun
Alights upon the Michaelmas,
Adorning sills with ivy strung.

The pulpit decked with greenery
Festooned with berries red and bright.
Whilst golden leaves trail to the floor,
Adding their magic to this sight.

We celebrate with crops and flowers
Another year with blessing crowned.
A partnership with rain and sun
Where farmers work the fertile ground.

August

August

Sandcastles

We hunted for buckets to take to the beach,
And there we built castles the tide could not reach.

Our parents in deckchairs were happy to doze
After finding a rock pool and dipping their toes.

An occasional eye on us kids as we played.
We were proud of the beautiful castles we made.

We dug a long trench, then went searching for shells...
A frequent mistake as each sand-digger tells...

For given an hour or two, waves on the turn
Had filled up the trenches. (When will youngsters learn?)

Our wobbly sandcastles soon fell flat and small,
And very soon nothing was left there at all.

The rock pools were soon under water quite deep.
Good job that our folks hadn't fallen asleep –

As deckchairs and rugs had to be quickly moved
For the tide was relentless, the hours had now proved.

But, not to be daunted, we'll come back again
To build more sandcastles – we just don't know when.

There are so many lessons to learn at the beach.
You can never build castles the tide cannot reach.

August

Inspiration

I am a small part of this world,
And I'm struck by its beauty and wealth.
Abundant in riches in water and rock
Where mysteries are buried for all to unlock,
And secrets await to discover by stealth.

I am a small part of this world
Where the mountains run down to the sea.
Where the heights that I climb and the depths that I trawl
Make me realise, how marvellous, being so small
Yet inspired by all nature, my spirit's set free.

I am a small part of this world,
And I'm physically challenged each day.
But surrounded by scenery, wild and untouched,
That fills me with awe that I value so much,
I'm inspired to feel blessed, there is no better way.

August

Home

Home is where I wash behind the ears
And leave a dirty rim around the bath.
Home is where the telephone sheds tears
Of sadness and of joy, the aftermath.

Home is where the garden is a segment
Of nature; small, secret and undisturbed.
Where flowers jostle for the warmth of sunshine,
And I can lay and listen to the birds.

Home is where my hopes and dreams are nurtured,
Where care spills over on to all I touch.
I strive, I rest, relax. From ills I'm cured.
It's there I find the love I need so much.

August

A Leisure Journal

1st August

2nd August

3rd August

4th August

5th August

6th August

7th August

August

8th August

9th August

10th August

11th August

12th August

13th August

14th August

A Leisure Journal

15th August

16th August

17th August

18th August

19th August

20th August

21st August

22nd August

23rd August

24th August

25th August

26th August

27th August

28th August

A Leisure Journal

29th August

30th August

31st August

Notes

August

Notes

A Leisure Journal

August 31st

The last warm day of August,
When thistledown blows on the breeze,
And Autumn is getting her paint-box out
To drizzle rust red on the leaves.

The stubble is rough to the walker's heel
As the barns are filled with hay.
The heat-haze shimmers from parched brown grass
Where the fox with her young would play.

Now the dew of the morn lies brightly
Till the shadows at length disappear.
And the blackberries burst with their juices,
Proclaiming that Autumn is near.

September

September

Time Flies

I guess in just a few week's time
The summer will have flown.
And brand new school kit shows how much
The children must have grown.

How silently their age creeps up
When summer turns to fall.
We hardly know where time has flown,
And were they young at all?

Oh yes, each line upon my face
And wrinkle on my brow
Shows how concerns of growing up
Have troubled me till now.

We cannot cosset or protect
The children in our care.
But give them all the love they need,
Good food and wholesome air.

Meanwhile, whilst they are at their desks
An empty silence falls.
How shall I fill each lonely hour
Within these homely walls?

Should I consider part-time work?
Re-join the general flow?
Or resurrect a previous skill?
Time on my hands seems slow.

Before I know it they'll have flown
To pastures new – and as for me?
I'll concentrate on how to spend
My new-found liberty!

September

A Leisure Journal

The Turning Wheels

O central orb 'round which we quietly turn
And unseen yet, our Maker for us yearns
As mankind does not learn from lessons past
And only craves for riches, power, fast.

But what goes round comes round again, we see
Great empires once, so little now they be.
For what we once exploited we now pay
And palaces in crumbling ruins lay.

Yet wheels can turn for progress and for gain,
Just look at transport with the cart or train.
All industry and recreation feel
Reliant on the turning of a wheel.

A perfect circle gives the smoothest ride.
The craftsman engineering this with pride.
Unlike man's evolved rise and fall,
Each revolution will sustain us all.

September

Caught Unawares

That biting bitter wind is here,
And finds the gap beneath the door.
It whistles in the unlit stove,
Then makes a dash across the floor.

When breezes skimmed across the heath,
Was Summer only here last week?
But now an icy shock takes hold
Of hat-less head and scarf-less cheek.

It's time to gather in the fruits,
A welcome bounty from the hedge,
Boil up the jam and make preserves
To stack along the pantry ledge.

Yet was it only days ago
I laid my head upon the sand
To feel the sunshine penetrate
Its final beams on face and hand?

But now we're off to fetch some logs
To light the stove, all glowing warm.
The wind has caught us unawares.
A fore-runner of Winter's storm.

September

A Leisure Journal

1st September

2nd September

3rd September

4th September

5th September

6th September

7th September

September

8th September

9th September

10th September

11th September

12th September

13th September

14th September

A Leisure Journal

15th September

16th September

17th September

18th September

19th September

20th September

21st September

September

22nd September

23rd September

24th September

25th September

26th September

27th September

28th September

A Leisure Journal

29th September

30th September

Notes

September

Notes

Special October

There is something special about the bird-song today;
Their piping wistfully, homing song.
Notes mellow or mourning the last dregs of autumn sun,
Before the short dark days enfold us in peace.
It's October.

There is something special about the hills today;
Their gentle wildness resting,
Basking velvet in the early evening rays
Before the blasts of winter make their slopes
Chap and wrinkle with rain channels.
It's October.

There is something special about my cottage today;
Windows flung wide before the winter seal.
Revelling in a late-blossom frame around the door
Its beauty to be hidden warm within till Spring.
It's October.

There is something special about the atmosphere today;
Last minute buzzing of the tired bee.
Crickets hug the wall before the street-lamps burn.
Like the sun's solstice,
Equal warmth and cold battling for supremacy.
It's October.

October

October

Taking Tea

It is quintessentially English
to take tea at half-past three.
With chores done and shopping over,
there is now some time for me.
Though jeans and crops and chinos
have replaced the gowns of lace
Which were lovely, yet impractical
on ladies full of grace.
For in days gone by, the privileged
sat sipping cups of tea,
But now this joy is open to
the likes of you and me.

And of course tomorrow morning
there'll be coffee with my friends,
It's amazing how each decade
has its socializing trends.
I like to see a table laid
with scones and jam and cake,
With serviettes and china
that you wouldn't want to break!
But usually it's just a mug,
with biscuits on my lap.
Surveying everything around,
before another nap.

October

The Town Hall Clock

Resolutely perched upon the roof,
Of steadfast pressing onward you're the proof.
Whilst in the rooms below, a Planning Trial,
Not showing on your non-commital dial,
Reflects the business of this seat of power.
Your business is to simply tell the hour,
Unsullied by the goings-on below.
From tax to benefits the problems flow.
And commerce sweeps along outside with pace,
Just glancing up to glimpse your stoic face.
And clerks amid their calculating sigh
To hear the homeward hour strike from on high.
The clock ticks on, and they pursue with haste
The homeward road without a moment's waste.
Although escaping screens they've 'worked' all day,
Beguiling leisure ones control their play.

October

Modelling

To replicate some thing to scale,
A dinosaur with scaly tail.
Intact with rig, a wooden boat.
(Or motorised, which stays afloat!)
A spitfire, hurricane or jet.
With skill and glue its pieces set.
All these with patience, we have tried
To stem the uncreative tide.

We are a nation I.T. mad,
And losing craft skills makes me sad.
Where individuals set the pace
We base it on another's face.
Their clothes, their hair, their money too
Develops into me and you.

So come on, let us make a stand.
OUR character to bring to hand.
By all means moulded on what's right,
Not what falls in the media's light.
Let's see what talents need some help
To venture from the darkened shelf.
Admired by others, what we've made
Will show the world the part we played.

October

A Leisure Journal

1st October

2nd October

3rd October

4th October

5th October

6th October

7th October

October

8th October

9th October

10th October

11th October

12th October

13th October

14th October

A Leisure Journal

15th October

16th October

17th October

18th October

19th October

20th October

21st October

October

22nd October

23rd October

24th October

25th October

26th October

27th October

28th October

A Leisure Journal

29th October

30th October

31st October

Notes

October

Notes

A Leisure Journal

November

Struggling to peer over nearby roofs,
And not quite clearing the fir tree's crown,
The sun still arks with failing strength,
And cold nights beckon its going down.

All saints – witches – guys – Advent;
This grey month fills with expectancy.
Scurrying, storing for dark days ahead
The squirrel hides nuts 'neath the nearby tree.

The leafless sculptures are enhanced by
Car headlamps on darkening eves.
Strange shapes loom of the snapping twig
That once was covered brightly in autumn leaves.

November deadens as fireworks redden.
The bonfire smokes, the hearth burns warm.
I idly through the deep leaves scuff.
From the comfort of home it's hard to be torn.

As nature winds down in burrow and stem,
Would that man could wind down in November days
Before they become the December crush,
And he's lost his wits in the shopping maze.

November

November

A Leisure Journal

Room to be Me

There is room to be me when I'm here on my own.
I don't have to pick up the telephone.
The doorbell unanswered – I'm having a nap
And mustn't disturb the cat curled on my lap.

The dust goes unchecked – the cleaning is sparse.
Just sometimes I launch out on bushes and grass,
But it has to be warm with no nip in the air.
For all-weather gardening, I just couldn't care.

For music and poetry and reading a book
And things of the mind (but I do like to cook)
Are far more my scene when I'm here on my own
And there's room to be me, with no-one to moan.

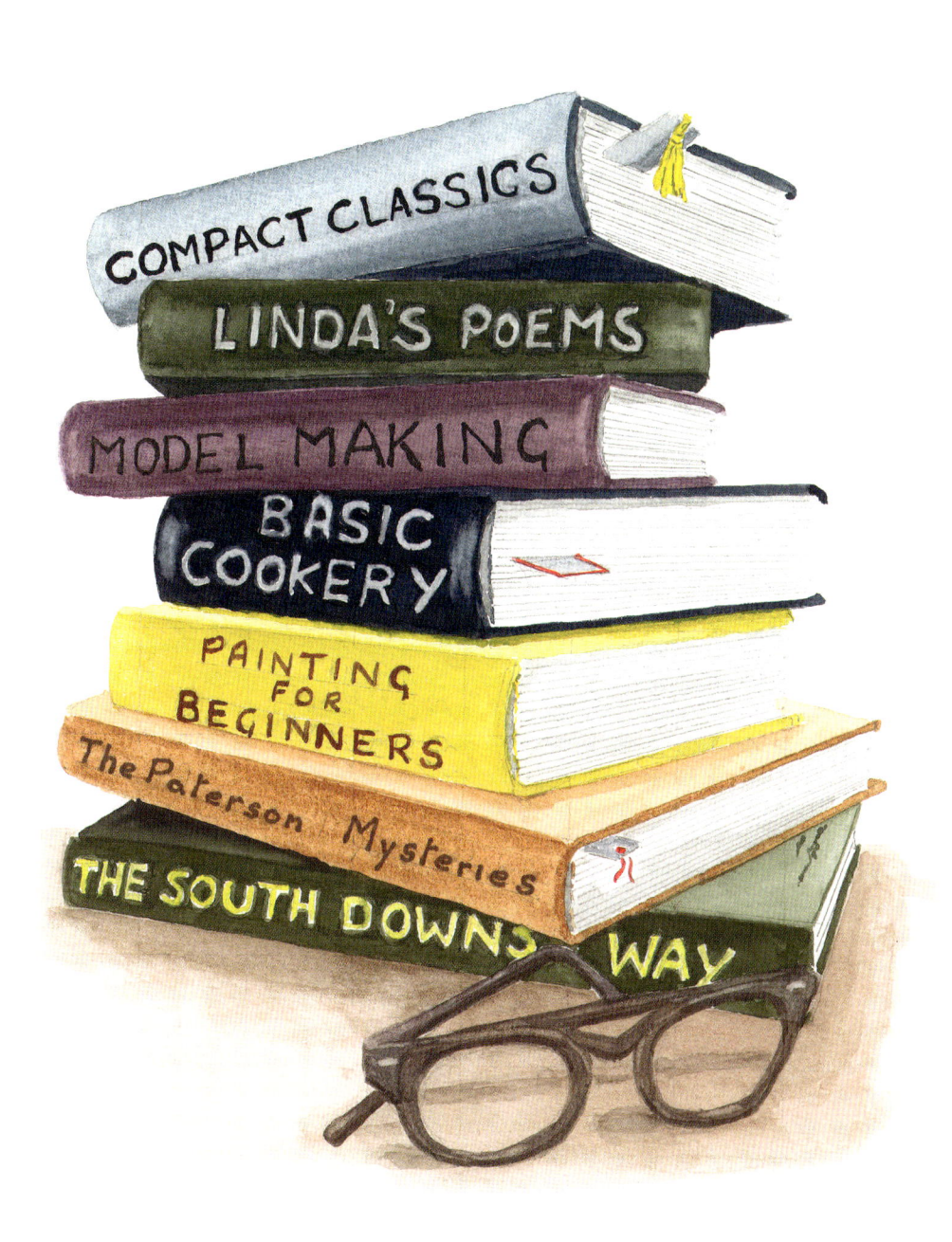

November

A Leisure Journal

The Choirmaster

You have the means to interpret the notes and phrases.
You dissect the chords and find the inner depth there.
Just what the composer set out to achieve, you trace,
And with your baton you guide us through the maze in the air.

You touch all our lives and make the music live.
How can we thank you enough for your training?
You grind us down, mould us and remake us
Into one glorious sound, making our souls sing.

When task is complete and you have given your all,
And the choir and the audience have reached the sublime,
We can unwind and slip back into homely comforts,
Slowly to descend from the musical peaks we climb.

*(Written in thankful appreciation of Laszlo Heltay,
Choral Director of Brighton Festival Chorus. 1968 – 1995)*

Some time has passed since you were once our guide.
I reminisce with longing and with pride
For what you taught, deep-rooted in my soul.
Our mentor, you played such a major role.
For thus inspired, dimensions passed pure 'fact',
As making music seemed a sublime act.

November

A Leisure Journal

The Busker

In my fiddle-case you'll find
Coin and copper from the kind.
Or an over bulging purse
Made you tip the weighty curse.
Whilst with tune upon my string,
Or with melody I sing,
Sits my dog with hearth-side ease,
Dreaming of the fire he leaves.
Just to keep me company
In my lonely symphony.
There we shelter in the door,
Making money for the poor.
Up the street our notes resound
From our pitch on frozen ground.
Let me pierce your broken heart.
In my music take your part.
Let your notes drop in my case.
One day you might take my place.

November

A Leisure Journal

1st November

2nd November

3rd November

4th November

5th November

6th November

7th November

8th November

9th November

10th November

11th November

12th November

13th November

14th November

A Leisure Journal

15th November

16th November

17th November

18th November

19th November

20th November

21st November

22nd November

23rd November

24th November

25th November

26th November

27th November

28th November

A Leisure Journal

29th November

30th November

Notes

November

Notes

A Birthday Challenge

It's somebody's birthday, the coming of light
We celebrate now with a festival bright.
There're carols and pantomimes, parties and games.
The sending of cards, (let me run through those names!)
There's buying a Christmas tree, fixing the lights,
And making sure candles will be burning bright.
There're presents and mince pies and warm Christmas pud.
With diets forgotten we'll tuck into food
As we herald the coming of one special boy,
And make sure each household can share in our joy.
But, let's not forget, as we enter our church
The meaning of Christmas, our hearts we must search.
And there, as we humbly kneel by stable door,
Does the birth of this infant STILL fill us with awe?

December

A Leisure Journal

Star Gazing

Minute, I gaze up at the heavens so still.
They are closer than breathing, on top of the hill.
This beautiful silence a part of me stirs.
And windless, below me, the dark of the firs.

If I reach out my hand can I grasp at your awe?
Can I pluck but one star to take home for my door?
Must I return homeward and shut you outside?
Can't I keep you for ever, in safety to hide…

To recapture your beauty, you spear of the night.
A wondrous perfection of brilliant white light
To pierce the long watches of dullness and gloom
When I must close the door and retire to my room?

With glass intervening and doors now tight shut,
The magic of outside from inside is cut.
The spell of the night has been broken in two
And each star in the dark now just part of the view!

December

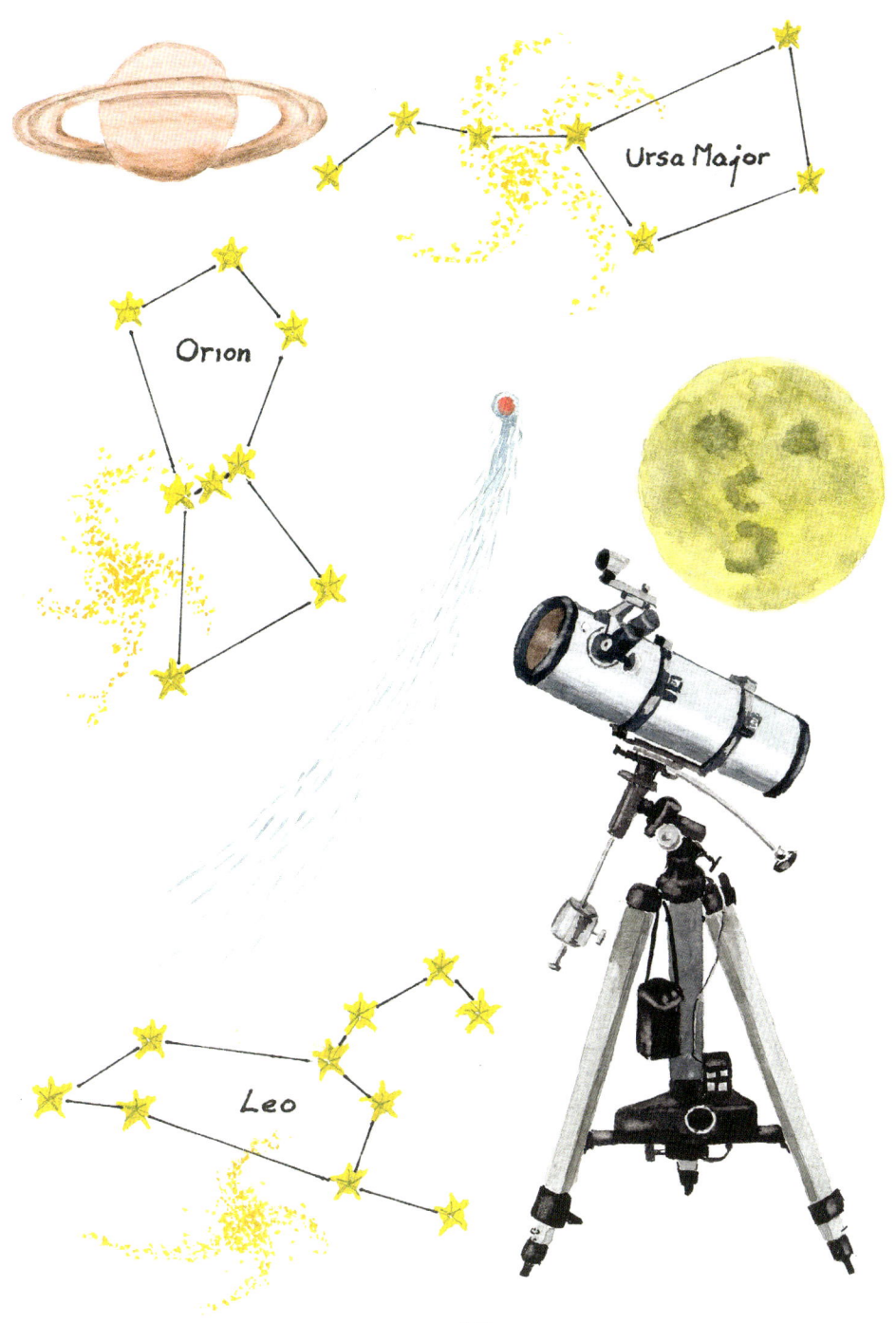

Ursa Major

Orion

Leo

A Leisure Journal

A Fantasy
About sixty ants stay awake to celebrate Christmas…

GiANT
ANT, ANThony
paid scANT regard to his
gigANTic sister ANTonia's
ANTics, as she donned a vibrANT
mANTle over her red velvet pANTs,
in a distANT shANTy, and flippANTly
mimmicked a pedANTic sANTa. Carrying
a lANTern she found in the pANTry, and wearing
an ANTique pendANT, she ANTicipated a good Christmas
rANT – importANT to her. ANThony meanwhile, skipped
the bANTer, and, jubilANT from his latest singing success,
triumphANTly joined his pleasANT choir, to sing cANTicles
and descANTs, sometimes a little discordANTly. The cANTankerous
choirmaster was not tolerANT of truANTs, but reluctANTly accepted
a gallANT, vagrANT, peasANT in the ranks, who could only chANT
the dominANT, with a radiANT face, and a resonANT tone, and bANTer
with ANThony an odd flippANT joke. ANTonia was quite nonchalANT
when it came to Christmas music, tANTermount to bored, singing about
a recumbANT infANT. So, reliANT on her toy elephANT for company,
she gallANTly visited all the distANT village infANTs instead, and took
the
grandANTs,
(in her protuberANT
port-mANTeaux,)
posies of piquANTly
fragrANT chrysANTs
to brighten up their
mANTlepieces.

166

December

Thoughts on Christmas

Choral pranks.
Giving thanks.
Gather holly.
Feeling jolly.
Deck the Church.
Present search.
Fever pitch.
Poor and rich.
Cold distresses.
Time presses.
Chosen gifts.
Gloom lifts.
Parcel up.
Festive cup.
Food galore.
Crowded store.
Starry nights.
Manger sights.
Midnight bells.
Turkey smells.
Lights that flash.
Strapped for cash.
Visit friends.
Discourse mends.
Ponder deep.
Fall asleep.

December

A Leisure Journal

1st December

2nd December

3rd December

4th December

5th December

6th December

7th December

8th December

9th December

10th December

11th December

12th December

13th December

14th December

A Leisure Journal

15th December

16th December

17th December

18th December

19th December

20th December

21st December

22nd December

23rd December

24th December

25th December

26th December

27th December

28th December

A Leisure Journal

29th December

30th December

31st December

Notes

December

Notes